TRIGGERS

A Student Counsellor's Poetic Journey

By

SIMON DRAKE

TRIGGER WARNING!

The content herein focuses on the themes of mental health including self harm, suicide, addiction, and child abuse.

Praise For Triggers

Just Music
"Thank you for your poem which hits the mark in the brief conversation we had, as you clearly know music is a fascinating phenomenon and reaches far and wide the breadth of human experience. Your words are so poignant and meaningful in betraying this so thank you very much for sharing!" (Oscar Lotis, Music therapist)

Communicate
"That's so beautiful and aptly put. Thanks for sharing your poem I really appreciate it, that you were able to put yourself in my shoes and express this so eloquently too. Please let me know when you publish this as I would love to share this on social media channels and share how my presentation made you think and be aware of the barriers and journeys, we deaf people take!" Victoria Nelson, Counsellor, therapist and founder of deaf4deaf.com

I Want to Tell You Something
"I feel quite a large chunk of my own experience in that, I was shunned for quite a while when I was outted and I wasn't ready, so I was alone, scared and in denial! It's like that poem was written to be a reflection of out-casted pain! The first half I thought was beautiful but the second half I resonated with!" Carrie Bull, Third Dan Karate Black Belt Instructor and Firefighter.

Teenager
"The word flow is marvellous; the poem was able to reference the cruelty of social politics within teenagers without being over handed and how that cruelty can give way to traumatic experiences. The poem was able to illustrate the agony of being an outsider, which in turn leads to the questioning of their own worth. Despite its dark undertone, it ends with a comforting reminder that they don't have to be alone in their struggles and that encourages teens to reach out!" Catherine Julia, Author House.

Hoarding
"Wow, wow, wow, I'm blown away. I'm not sure I can convey my feelings into words, so moved by your poetry, what a gift!" Julieanne Steel, Clutter Therapist & Integrative Counsellor.

About The Author

Drowning in loss and depression, struggling to function and running on empty. That is where I found myself in December 2016. I was suffering and trapped in a void. Experiencing several life changing losses, over an extremely short period of time, left me feeling broken. I was in a very dark and lonely place and struggling to process my grief. Personal therapy over the proceeding twelve months helped to start shedding a little light back into my world. Beam by beam, I began to recover. During the therapeutic process my counsellor planted an idea: *"Have you ever thought about becoming a counsellor, you have the necessary tools, I think that you would be very good!"*. I was intrigued. Professionally I was going nowhere, working for a pound note with no real purpose, fulfilment, or job satisfaction. I signed up for an introduction to counselling course, and that was the first step that brought me to where I am now. Course by course, year by year, I worked tirelessly to achieve my goal of becoming a qualified therapist. Here I am, in July 2023, having completed my Diploma in Gestalt Therapy. It has been an amazing, challenging, rewarding, and life changing experience. During the process of completing my qualification, I started to write poetry which in turn has opened many other creative doors. In the last six months, I have had poetry published in five anthologies, been a guest on 'The Lewistry podcast' on Spotify, played a hitman in an indie movie 'Cochon and The Small Reset,' and regularly perform my work at Spoken Word Poetry events in London. I am extremely grateful, for the many opportunities, which I have been afforded. I now look to the future with hope and excitement for what lies ahead. It's amazing what a little time and healing can do!

Author's Poems already Published, 2023:

Mum, Lucidity and *Thrown Away*, have all been published on Spillwords.com
Teenager, Bullied and *Self-Harm*, are in *Suicide* (Vol. 2). (Published by Poetry for Mental Health)
Drink or Two, Arcade, Addiction, Playing Tricks and *The Dragon* are in *Addiction*. (Published by Poetry for Mental Health)
Monster, Reconnect, Mask and *Drowning in Sadness* are in *Mental Health*. (Published by Poetry for Mental Health)
Toy has been published in *Wheelsong Poetry Anthology* (Vol.3).

Introduction

"Minding my own business, plodding along on my journey to becoming a qualified counsellor, when four months into the diploma course in Gestalt Therapy I was read a poem by our guest speaker, Paula Mates, called My Child Within, written by Kathleen Algoe. I wrote a poem called Lost Child as part of a creative task and haven't been able to stop writing poetry since.

This book is my first and comes with a Trigger warning, the content is powerful and might take you to places that may Trigger you. The journey I have been on over the last two years is one of truth and self-discovery, giving you, the reader an insight into my creative soul."

Simon Drake, November, 2023.

E: 19.simondrake.74@gmail.com
FB: @simon.drake.568
Instagram: @simondrake8120
YouTube: @simondrake7092

You Are Not Alone

If you are, or someone you know is, struggling, here are a few of the many organizations that offer advice and support. You are not alone: do not be afraid to reach out if you feel you need to.

Samaritans; call 116 123 or email jo@samaritans.org
Mind; call 0300 123 3393 or email info@mind.org.uk
Shelter; call 0300 330 1234 or email info@shelter.org.uk
Alcoholics Anonymous London; call 0800 9177 650 or email help@aamail.org
Mosaic Counselling; call 01727 863 224 or email help@mosaiccounsellingservices.com

Contents

TRIGGERS

A Student Counsellor's Poetic Journey

Triggers

Thank you for picking me up
Not so fast, don't put me down
You've got your foot in my poetic door
Why not have a good look around

I am sure here within these pages
There is something that might trigger you
Have a flick through my book
Have a look at the pictures
Why not read a poem or two

I aim to inspire, I can't promise to please
This books not an itch you can scratch
The poems I have written
Delve back through your memories
You may find the perfect match

Don't get distracted, turn off your devices
Take some time to have a look through
If you are honest, I have no doubt in my mind
You will find a poem written just for you.

Hiding

I would love to know what you're thinking
Yes, you hiding over there
Your point of view I would love to hear
Are you brave enough to share

Your opinion really matters
Your perspective may shed some light
I wondered why you won't engage
Are you stuck in fight or flight

Is it because you are nervous
Perhaps it's because you are shy
I believe you could really contribute
But you won't and I wondered why

There is no need to feel awkward
You are, I see the signs
Many have felt the way that you do
You'll find your voice in time.

There's no need to feel pressured
When you're ready the words will come
You have come so far just being here
The healing has already begun

Just Music

Just music you say
Where did you get that idea
Please explain it like I am stupid
You need to make this clear
Don't you have feelings
Do you not have a soul
Have you never heard a song before
That made you lose control
A song pulling on your heartstrings
Reminding you of love
That they were something special

A gift from up above
Just music you say
What did music ever do to you
Did it make you feel neglected
What kind of trauma did it put you through
Can you name it out loud
Is it written in a song
Be brave enough to tell me
Where you both went wrong

Music is forgiving
I promise, it would never hold a grudge
Go and ask it out to play
It'll fill your heart with love
See it's not just music
It's life's beat made just for you
Lay back relax and listen to it
It will make your dreams come true

Message in a Bottle

I put a message in a bottle
I watched it drift on out to sea
The tide took it from my hands
Something so personal to me

My thoughts I had written
I signed it from a friend
Will the message wonder aimlessly
Will a watery grave become its end

I lost sight of the bottle
As the waves came crashing in
My feet sank deep into the sand
My face kissed by the sea wind

I turned to walk away
Then stopped for one last glance
Thinking that maybe one day
It will reach someone, however slim the chance

Many, many years later
The message was read, my wish came true
It reached a stranger and we connected
It is so nice to finally meet you

Meet up for Coffee?

Why ask for us to meet up
When you have no intention to
Pretending to miss my company
I would just prefer the truth
It would be really great to see you
I have got so many things I want to say
Let's meet up in the coming weeks
I will call to arrange a day

I'm so tired of the bullshit
I am no longer hanging on
I've heard this from you many times
You're playing the same old song
It really used to hurt me
Being let down was difficult to bare
I would look forward to meeting you
I guess that's because I cared

Those days are long gone
Now I could not care less
In fact, don't bother contacting me
It feels great getting this off my chest
Once bitten twice shy you see
Never again will you make a fool of me
The corridor of uncertainty
No longer part of my vocabulary

Now for you, I'm never free
For a catch-up over a coffee
I can no longer spare a text
Don't contact me it is for the best
Thank you for the lesson though
I will never forget its worth
Teaching me to be treated with respect
Is the least that I deserve.

Communicate

Each day the same as the last
I struggle to hear you
I know I'm not being heard
I can't stand this, I am so frustrated
You are speaking, I can't hear a word
Silence drives me insane
Hello, I'm talking to you
What, because I'm deaf, am I to blame

Having feelings, you cannot imagine
You can't relate
I want to share them with you
How can we communicate
I am so angry
I want to scream that out
I won't hear its sound
So I stay silent

Even though I want to scream and shout
My confidence left me long ago
Being replaced with hopelessness, self-doubt
They're not my friends, although they try to pretend
Squatting rent free in my mind
I want them kicked out, left behind
Can we work together
Could you please be patient and kind
Talk slowly so I can lip read you
One word at a time and ever so slowly

We can converse, we can communicate
Understanding one another
I think we're beginning to relate
Thank you, it's been wonderful
Finally feeling heard, by spreading the word
Talking, writing, or even signing
Giving me the opportunity, to feel connected
After all this time, of feeling neglected, rejected
That's all I ever wanted, to be heard for who I am
A person to be loved and respected.

Missing Pieces

So, you have made your mind up
That is so unfair
Pieces of the jigsaw are missing
My story hasn't had the chance to air

I feel really disappointed
Your actions have hit a nerve
I should be able to express myself
It's the least that I deserve

Preconceived judgements
What, are we back at school
If the situation was reversed
I'd want to hear what happened from you

This relationship is not for me
50/50 is a must
I cannot be myself around you
Good foundations are built on trust

Perhaps if you ever grow up
On others opinions, you wouldn't rely
You'd be able to make your own mind up
Then I wouldn't be saying goodbye.

The Serpent

Laying with a serpent
You do not realise you are, oblivious
Completely unaware of the impending danger
The threat upon your life

The serpent's cunning, patient
Still in the long grass, with stealth they move
Sensitive to the plights of the weak, the vulnerable
In the herd, you stand out

Naive like a new-born
Your warning signs disabled
They place themselves beside you
Danger signs removed, silently

The serpent slowly begins to coil
Removing family and friends
From view and earshot
Now it is just you two
The victim and the serpent

Totally unaware of how manipulative
Persuasive they can be
The serpent has you
You question your own sanity
The coil tightens

You are in their clutches
Impending mortal danger,
Isolated, the coil tightens
As the abuse begins.

Weekly Visit

Visiting you is painful
Yet every week I come
It does not matter if it is raining
Or I am greeted with the sun
I never really know what to say
It's a struggle to find the words
Sometimes I leave the talking
To the singing of the birds

Even when I do talk
I always seem to cry
Sharing my devastation
I speak without reply
It is not a place for conversations
Or a place to meet
Even though I see familiar faces
A smile and nod are how we speak

I'd give anything to hear your voice
To hold your hand in mine
These are the thoughts I share with you
It is how I pass the time
Words can't express how much I miss you
Things just haven't been the same
I can't believe it's been seven years
Since I heard you say my name

I will see you next week
It's time to leave the cemetery
I feel connected to you
Knowing, you watch over me
My love for you grows stronger
I feel your warmth within my heart
Even though you're here no longer
We will never be apart.

Thrown Away

I've had my heart broken and dreams shattered
I have wished I was no longer here
Crushed and tossed into the garbage
I meant nothing and now that's so clear

Why did you play with my feelings
Use me then throw me away
Discarded with no thought of the consequences
That scar still stings to this today

I was left to pick up the pieces
The devastation I faced on my own
Bricks and mortar, this place has no soul
A house that's no longer my home

I never listened to my gut feeling
I broke an unwritten rule
Alarm bells were ringing loud and clear
My reflection shows the tears of a fool

So many years have passed me by
My heart feels like it still needs to mend
I deserve better but life doesn't work that way
I wonder will I ever love and feel love again

Forgiveness

I wonder how long you waited
To pass that loaded gun
Those you used were inconsequential
So long as you could have your fun

As you watched the gun go off
A blind man could see your glee
The casualties just the price of war
As you began your attack on me

So, you spoke without reply
Revealing who you really are
Your deepest darkest thoughts exposed
I'm so glad you went that far

You cannot un-speak those words
They can't be taken back
Your real self, revealed to all
Your facade has begun to crack

Yet it is you who I feel sorry for
I can see that you're in pain
You cannot hide who you are inside
Your life's a crying shame

I will do what you cannot
Blessed with knowing right from wrong
It is you who's trapped with hate and guilt
So I will forgive you and move on.

Never Coming Home

See you in the evening love
Have a wonderful day
I love you more than life itself
I had better be on my way

I have such a busy day ahead
My office is the road
A lorry driver for many years
I was made for it I suppose

I like working on my own
It gives me time to think
To sing along to my favourite songs
Or listen to a podcast link

I cannot believe the weather though
It's wet with heavy fog
As usual idiots are driving way too fast
It's raining cats and dogs

A biker has just cut me up
I am scared, I've lost my nerve
I have lost control of my lorry
I have no choice but to swerve

With all the water on the road
I can't keep my lorry in its lane
The brakes are failing I have no traction
I am beginning to aquaplane

The artic is tipping onto its side
I have lost control
Right now, I'm absolutely terrified
The rig has begun to roll

My family flashed before my eyes
It was such a weird sensation
I am no longer scared, content and calm
Headed for the central reservation

That's the last thing I remembered

Feeling love and I'm not alone
The A13 where my journey ended
I am never going home

I passed that accident this morning
Then read later, the driver had died
I am also a lorry driver by trade
His loss brought tears to my eyes

Be mindful when you're on the roads
Being sensible can save a life
All road users should get home safely
Please watch your speed when you drive.

Muddied Waters

Would you like a little silence
I am sensing you need a little space
You just don't seem to want me
It is written on your face

I really don't want to lose you
Yet I feel like I already have
Is it too late to save us I wonder
When you have put us in the past

How can I really show you
Tell me what to do to make you stay
Actions speak louder than words
I will act on whatever words you say

If it's just a misunderstanding
Why is the gap between us now so far
My love for you is unconditional
I accept you for who you really are

I forgive you and I love you
Can you not do the same
Do not let pride muddy our waters
Please don't put out our flame

How on earth did we get to this
When did silence became the way we talk
We used to be such great communicators
Can we try again before you walk.

Mum

(Tribute to Shahin's son Kalu)

From here in heaven I see you
The woman that you have become
I wish that you could hear my voice
I am so proud to be your son
I know how much you've missed me
I hear every word you say
I know how much you love me Mum
I kneel beside you when you pray
My love for you is limitless
Infinite, until the end of time

Mum you'll always be my everything
So loving and so very kind
Bursting with pride as I watch you
There's no limit to what you can achieve
A qualified counsellor, what a journey
When you doubted I always believed
You have such a way about you
Although we're now worlds apart
Words cannot describe how proud I am
For all eternity you have my heart
Such strength, you're truly amazing
Just once, I wish you could see
Your accomplishments are extraordinary
What will be, will always be

Heartbreak has been two heavy buckets
That you've carried, grieving for me
Close your eyes Mum and picture
Pouring them both into the sea
The time to be sad is now over
Mum this is a birthday wish
When you feel the wind on your cheeks
It's me sending a son's loving kiss
I want you to enjoy yourself
I'm with you every step of the way
I want you to be at peace and happy
Fulfil my wishes mum on my birthday

Mother's Message to her Son

(Tribute to Shahin's son Kalu)

I know this will never reach you
But I will write it all the same
I need to put my feelings down
I need to share this pain
My son you never heard me
Words, lost on their way to you
I loved you more than life itself
Something that you never knew

Born from me, my purest love
My sunset over the sea
My ray of light in the darkest sky
You were the air I breathed
Nothing has ever been written
To describe my love for you
But the depth of it is infinite
Yet you never even knew

I longed for a connection
I felt we had drifted far apart
I wanted a conversation with you
To explain you always had my heart
How cruel that you were taken
Life is so incredibly unfair
I will never know if you ever knew
Just how much I really cared

It has been three years now
These wounds will never heal
I've had to come to terms with this
And the emptiness I feel
I think about you in every second
My mind and heart have no relief
Before I sleep, I pray for you
Still, I've not found any peace

Hours and hours thinking
Wishing I could change the past
Hoping to hold you in my arms again
With a hug that would forever last

I know you're looking down on me
At times I feel your presence in the room
What's the view like from up there son
Amongst the stars and moon

Bitterness and anger
Swallowed me up in a raging sea
Any bad feelings between us son
No longer have a hold on me
I love you boy with all my heart
In heaven we will meet again
Just know I miss you everyday
So pay me a visit, every now and then.

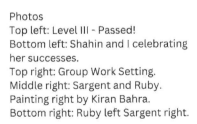

Photos
Top left: Level III - Passed!
Bottom left: Shahin and I celebrating her successes.
Top right: Group Work Setting.
Middle right: Sargent and Ruby.
Painting right by Kiran Bahra.
Bottom right: Ruby left Sargent right.

Caged

I look with sadness in my heart
You're no longer who you used to be
Your joy for life and impulsive nature
Has been quelled, to be with me

I feel so guilty, it really burns
Seeing the sacrifices you have made
This version of you is an empty shell
A price you shouldn't have to pay

I know I can't live with this
Something so beautiful, trapped in a cage
Guilt has engulfed my very soul
Witnessing how much you've had to change

I've made a decision although it's painful
This relationship wasn't meant to be
The person I loved isn't who you are
For us both I am setting you free.

The Tree

Have you noticed how barren a tree can look in the wintertime, standing naked and alone in the cold. The branches reaching up to the heavens asking how has it come to this. How have I lost all that made me so beautiful, I had thousands of leaves that made me look magnificent and covered me.

The flowers and leaves that bloomed from my branches added to my splendour, now here I stand without all that made me great, without all that made me stand out, without all that made me, me.
A whisper in the wind spoke to her, the tree that thought she had lost everything.

Look how strong and resilient you are in the harshest winter, with all that you thought supported you and made you so beautiful gone, carried off with the changing of the seasons. Yet here you remain steadfast in the toughest of circumstances.

That is your strength, the base of your power, all you need are the right conditions and you will once again be magnificent.
You need to endure the bitterness of winter, then as the season slowly progresses into spring the darkness will lift from your weary branches.

Even the misery of relentless rain is needed to help nourish the deepest roots that connect you to the earth. You will feel something happening a change you cannot explain, once again you will feel the warmth of the sun and light that it brings.

Shifting shadow that you have been standing in for far too long, beams shining upon you once more. Now you will be able to grow, confident, reassured as we move into summertime. The old you is returning, the leaves are here to cover your naked body, the flowers have returned to bloom.

Yet there has been a change in your exterior that provides your cover, your shelter and confidence that makes you, you.
It is different, it has adapted as you have had to adapt, this is what happens in life when you feel you are at your strongest, at your most beautiful and magnificent then lose yourself as she lost all that made her, her.

Remember it took three things to be able to transform once again from the shadow of her former self back to the sight that makes you stop and look in awe.

Appreciating her beauty, to sit in the shade she has provided on a beautiful summers afternoon. It took warmth to give her the confidence to once again to be able to bloom, it took the rays of the sun to chase away the darkness she had sat in for far too long and most importantly it took time.

Whenever we are at our lowest point, the combination of these three elements can heal and help to once again grow many different forms of life, like this tree for example.

Money

It is only money after all
Causing so much trouble and strife
When the penny drops, you realise it's worth
Only then will you find value in life

Love, family, relationships and kindness
Where you will find all of your wealth
Money cannot buy happiness
It doesn't even guarantee good health

Bank accounts and postcodes
Expensive cars all parked on the drive
Millionaires can also be miserable
Money allows jealousy to thrive

You can never have enough money
You see the Jones' are keeping score
If wealth is your God, you've missed the point
The value of life is worth so much more

Ending up the richest in the graveyard
What a wasted life you've had
Prioritising money over love and happiness
Those who stand to inherit won't be sad

The gift of life is a blessing
Love and Happiness make you rich as can be
Don't waste your life on materialistic things
Trust your feelings that is the key

I Want to Tell You Something

I say all the right things not to standout
I do not want the spotlight on me
The last thing I need is being backed into a corner
Exposing all my vulnerabilities
It's a battle for me to fit in to this world
There is a war raging within
I feel so uncomfortable, wearing this mask
I am self-conscious in my own skin
I have known for a while that I'm different
There's something that needs confessing

How do I tackle the elephant in the room
I'm so sensitive, constantly second guessing
I have never liked who my friends like
I think I'm in love with a friend
I've buried these feelings deep down inside
It's been driving me around the bend
I am not really sure how to broach this
The subject of my sexuality
I am terrified of the implications
Being rejected by my friends and family

I really do want to come out
Ending this façade once and for all
I am scared and that fear is holding me back
God, this is such a tough call
I am so fed-up with all of the acting
I want to come out I don't want to hide
I want to scream from the top of my lungs
I'm gay and say it with pride
What's the worst that could happen
I could be kicked out, I could be disowned
I already feel so sad and miserable
Carrying this all on my own
Deep breath, I will face the music
I'll be courageous, facing demons within
Mum, Dad have you got a minute
Sit down I want to tell you something

Misunderstood

So easy to misread a situation
How many times have you misheard the words
to a song
Singing the wrong lyrics for years and years
Before realising that you'd got them wrong
That's the thing with communication
Making sure you're on the same page
It's frustrating when you're misunderstood
Invoking feelings of anger and rage

Do not be afraid to say, Sorry
I want to make sure I've got this right
Is that what you said and meant when you spoke
Before insinuations have the chance to take flight
Feuds can last an eternity
If only all parties showed understanding
You can end up not talking for decades
Because of a misunderstanding

Be patient make sure there is clarity
When important things you have to say
Certain that context and facts have been understood
And that's what's been taken away
It's of the upmost importance
The message is understood between you and me
A crucial fact about a peaceful life
Communication and clarity are absolute key

My Everything

You are my coffee in the morning
My shower that washes over me
Everything that's good in life
That's what you are, you see

You are my absolute everything
I don't know where to start
What I do know with certainty
Is you are the beating of my heart

You are my every good choice
Every right thing I've ever done
The moon that lights up my night sky
By day you're my shinning sun

You've always been my leading lady
In every movie that I see
My favourite song on repeat
I carry your love around with me

You could've had any man you wanted
Yet you chose me to make you mine
If I had a million picks at love
I would pick you every time

We have got our lives to live
I am going to love you until I die
I will always give you all of me
My home is by your side

You really are my everything
My love story has come true
Every day for me is Christmas Eve
Because I get to spend that day with you.

Bullied

I am constantly bullied, it's never ending
Every minute of every hour of everyday
I can't go on, I'm contemplating suicide
I feel like there's no other way

My anxiety's a ticking timebomb
I can't cope, I'm about to explode
I have got no one and nowhere to turn to
I can't take it, I need to unload

I am the butt of the "IT crowds" jokes
They laugh as I breakdown and cry
Their comments, stab me like bee stings
It is relentless, I'm broken inside

WhatsApp, I avoid like the plague
On Facebook I am ridiculed too
On Instagram I'm constantly hounded
I'm lost, I don't know what to do

I can't face much more of this torture
I don't have a future, everything's bleak
My parents know something's wrong
I've lost my voice but I'm desperate to speak

I can't go on, I've had enough
I don't know how much longer I can last
I need help, can anybody hear me
I need help but I'm too scared to ask.

I See You

I see you for what you don't say
Not what you do
I see you for what you hide
Not what you share
I see you
Connecting in silence
Through conversations without substance
I see you
In the pain that you mask
Not the smile you present
I see you
For the tears you hold
Behind the laughter that flows
I see you

Not for the shoes that you wear
But the path you have walked
I see you
For whom you really are
Not who you think you should be
I see you
In your actions and deeds
Not your words of promise
I see you
When you don't want to be seen
For the fear of not being heard
Like hide and seek
There is a fear and excitement
In being found and being seen
No matter how well you hide
I see you.

Girls Night Out

Can't you just take the hint
Do I really have to be impolite
You're stepping on my very last nerve
I think it's time you said goodnight
I have no interest in your opinions
You are invading my personal space
I can see that you have no self-respect
Overconfidence is definitely misplaced

No, I don't want to hear your story
No, you're the one with an attitude
It's clear you are lacking humility
It's unattractive that you're so rude
We came out for a girl's night
Not that it's got anything to do with you
Those seats look really comfortable
Go over there and take a pew

You want to know if I have a boyfriend
Is it convenient that he's not here
What he doesn't know won't hurt him, right
That's what you said so let us be clear
Now comes the aggressive behaviour
You are so unbelievably predictable
I guess your egos taken a massive hit
Now you can't even be civil

Whoops here come the bouncers
You can't say you haven't been warned
You have heard that saying haven't you
Be careful of a woman scorned
When a woman says no, she means it
You can be rejected and still be polite
See you later sunshine
Enjoy the rest of your night

Addict

Junkie is such a dirty word
As filthy as the crap I use
The journey I take just to escape
So I can forget the abuse
I am stuck in a hole to be honest
It feels like a bottomless pit
I've had enough, I can't take anymore
I'm just so sick of it
I don't know where to turn to
At a dead end, I'm really stuck

Blanked when asking for help
I'm ignored, I've run out of luck
Burning too many bridges
I've let so many people down
Constantly treading water, I'm tired
I need help or else I will drown
Every now and then became a habit
In rough crowds I had to mix

Doing anything to find the cash I needed
I had to, to get my fix
I even robbed my own family
That is how I was disowned
I am to blame for this mess that I'm in
That's why I am all on my own
I have broken so many promises
Saying I want to make amends
Cravings takes hold, I can't think straight
The needle becomes my only friend

You walk past me, like I am nothing
On the streets I just don't exist
If I ended up dead in a squat
I don't think I'd even be missed
Please give me one more chance
You can see in the tears that I cry
I have to kick this habit, I'm desperate
If I don't, I know that I'll die

Can You Do Me A Favour

Hey, you, I know it's been a while
Could you please do a favour for me
Show a little interest in a girl
I would appreciate it immensely
She is beautiful with a free spirit
What you get is what you see
She's the prettiest thing, a tomboy
With a fantastic personality

Take the time to get to know her
Likes and loves, you already know
She would think the world of you
If a little interest you would show
You know her name already
She's something to behold
Polite and very quirky
Take her out she'd be happy to go

I shouldn't have to ask you
You need help jogging your memory
This pretty thing is your daughter
Remember the little girl, you had with me
When was the last time you called her
You don't see her face when you let her down
Not there to comfort or hold her
What's needed when you don't come around

I am not asking for any other reason
Both losing out, I need you to see
You are an important part of her life
Yet there's a hole where her father should be
Neither of you will get this time back
Are you willing to make amends
It's not fair, you keep breaking her heart
It's up to you how this story ends.

Cease Fire

Peace, you gave me that, I am still grateful even now.
The treaty signed in a hug and tears shed, I never thought it possible,
my anger was winning the battle, supported in the trenches by
frustration and stubbornness.

Peace, a word for the weak, for gutless cowards and traitors, not for
warriors, not for the just, those that will not budge an inch. Once they
feel they have been wronged, a war will rage, injustice the battle cry.

All contact cut off, reasoning and understanding held hostage with
forgiveness. Prisoners locked up without trial, casualties of war held
between two factions that won't communicate, an impasse

Have you noticed the altercation between the two parties only lasts a
few minutes, yet the ramifications set in, like ticks sucking all rationality
from you. You then play it over and over and over again, wounding
yourself on each viewing, playing this out for an eternity, there is no
escape.

Every waking hour spent at war, even in sleep the battle rages,
now the target has changed, the blows are self-inflicted.
Death by a thousand cuts, until out of nowhere an apology appears.
You were not expecting it, you did not even want to cross paths.
Sharing the same air and the sheer sight of them made you want to
vomit.

An apology has been offered, common sense greets it first
followed by reasoning and understanding, then finally forgiveness.
They know the damage caused; they have all borne witness,
they want this war to end. Within primarily, that happens by your
outwardly actions, an apology has been offered, I am sorry too, followed
by a flood of emotions.

A release, a relief, a huge weight lifted, at last real peace again.
Thank you, thank you, thank you. The irony is your mind is free to think
on something new. Now what on earth will you do with all that free
thinking time, rejoice in peace for starters.

Christian Name

The look in your eyes, the day they were born
An unbreakable bond, instantly formed
Your flesh, your blood, your heart, your soul
What you needed, making you whole

Promises made, for you to keep
To do no harm, never seeing them weep
Your priorities changed they will come first
Where did it go wrong the bubble has burst

To scar them so, those cuts are deep
Their love for you, has begun to seep
No longer the hero, you make them sad
How could you do that, they call you dad

Those little girls, to be seen but not heard
When you scream at their mother, they hear every word
When hitting her, psychologically you've hitting them too
Permanent damage, no excuses from you

Covered in bruises, repeatedly abusing their mum
Can you make amens for the damage you've done
The relationships over, promises irretrievably broken
Too late for empty words of apologies spoken

How will you feel, hearing your Christian name
Your daughters never calling you daddy again.

Complicated

Why is life so complicated
I don't get it, I go with the flow
Nothing has ever been easy for me
I guess that's why I'm feeling so low

Struggling with absolutely everything
I've never felt good enough
Trying my best and I'm not appreciated
Making my life unbelievably tough

I am lost, I have lost my identity
Trying to please all those around me
I'm worse off now than ever before
I don't remember who I used to be

How did I get on this merry go round
I am fed up I want it to stop
The voice in my head has had enough
Wanting me to just shut up shop

Maybe things will get better
A white lie I know that I'm fibbing
I'll get out of this mess; I am sure I will
No, I won't, who an earth am I kidding.

Purest Love

I smile whenever I think about you
It is a feeling words cannot describe
I loved you before I even met you
You have given meaning to my life

I get lost looking into your eyes
I hang on your every word
Wrapped around your little finger
This feeling is absurd

I don't have the same feelings for my partner
She will have to accept it because it is true
This is the purest love I have ever felt
My heart and soul belong to you

Other women now all mean nothing
No one will ever be in your league
With me by your side throughout your life
There's nothing you cannot achieve

I will give you everything I have and more
In life you'll have every opportunity
Nourished with every ounce of my love
My daughter you mean the world to me.

Paradise

Where your desires are met
Dreams are fulfilled
Every pleasure sampled
Where your mind is quiet
The sea is so calm
The beach is golden
The sand is fine, pure, unspoiled
You look out into the bluest ocean
That noise, the unmistakable sound
The sea kissing the shore

As it comes in and then goes out
Again and again, forever
You can sit there for hours
Totally entranced at peace
The sun so bright and warm
Not one speck of white in the sky
The breeze enough so you are comfortable
Without disturbing the sand
Where a minute is a lifetime
Your mind can now settle
Life is perfect
No devices, no distractions

A quiet mind, content
You are happy
If you want company
Then picture your guest
A friend, a loved one
Someone long gone
And they shall appear
You see them first
In the distance
Holding your hand above your eyes
To get a better look
Now you see them more clearly

As you make your way to each other
How long has it been
Holding one another close
Tears of joy and happiness

Roll down your cheeks
Time for hellos
Where is this place you ask
It is in your mind
Awaiting your company
Whenever you are ready to travel.

Childhood

When do you grow up, is it at 16 now that you can legally get married, you used to be able to leave school after your GCSEs and find yourself an income if you didn't fancy college. Is it at 17, now you have got your driver's licence and you can explore the world or as far as your little banger will take you.

Is it at 18, when so many things that are bad for you become legal, smoking, drinking and gambling. Perhaps it is 21, surely, you are no longer a child you are all grown up and armed and prepared to take on the world, with No Fear. How about 22, now studying has finally finished and you have a degree to boot.

Is it at 30, now you are married with a ring and certificate to confirm wedlock. Perhaps it's 40, there is no way you can still be a child with children of your own, halfway through your life the grey is starting to appear, what child has a bald spot or grey hair.

What child pays a mortgage and has all the responsibilities you have, if you are lucky, you might still be a child at 60 even though you are a grandparent your children are out making lives of their own, property, jobs, relationships, making their own way in the world.

Becoming an adult happens in two costly stages, the price is a heart-breaking toll that is almost too much to bare. When you lose your parents that is when your childhood ends, when you no can no longer be that little baby. When you are no longer reminded of the silly things you did by those that know you best, when you do not get that special cuddle anymore, that tells you everything is going to be okay.

When you cannot say dad there's something wrong with my car, can you look at it for me, can I borrow your tools dad, dad can I borrow some money I promise I will pay it back. When you can't have dad potter about in your garden and give you that much needed manley advice.

Mum put the kettle on, mum I cannot cope, mum what am I going to do, mum I need a cuddle from you. I feel so much better when you reassure me everything is going to be okay, partners cannot, no matter how hard they try fill that void.

You are no longer a child when you cannot be a child anymore, it is not by choice there is no special birthday, it just happens when you lose your parents and when that day comes your life will never be the same again.

Good Advice

I could really do with some of your advice
I took on board the guidance you would give
You were honest and thoughtful when you spoke
Straight to the point was your belief

A wise head on those shoulders
You had seen and done it all
That kind of experience cannot be bought
That is why I listened when you talked

Quietly you used to sit there
Enabling me to share how I felt within
I never felt judged or awkward with you
As you sat there processing

You held me as a baby
You were there to watch me grow
You guided me throughout my life
There was nothing you didn't know

I miss those egg and bacon sandwiches
Along with that lovely pot of tea
I love and miss you deeply, grandad
The only man that understood me, for me

Partners in Crime

Bullies have such wonderful personalities
Sargent filled my world with joy
Stealing my heart in the process
That's why there's such a void
No more running up the hallway
As I walk through the front door
Barking for attention
I won't hear that anymore
Smiling when I stroked you
Then you'd go and get a toy
An indestructible one supposedly
That in five minutes you'd destroy

Zooming like a Nutter
Running up and down
It's going to be so quiet now
Not having you around
Spoon fed for seven years
I think you had us on
Cakes and chocolates left unattended
In two seconds would be gone

Everywhere that I went
I'd look down and there you'd be
Partners in crime the two of us
You were the perfect foil for me
What about the dog walks
When you'd had enough, you sat
Holding onto the lead for dear life
Every time you saw a cat
I couldn't even sit alone
You would never let me be
You knew that your place in life
Was sat right next to me

Always up to mischief
When it was quiet alarm bells would ring
If you went missing for more than one minute
I knew you were up to something
Ten minutes we had to eat our dinners
Then the showing off would start

Hurry up I want some of that
Is what I heard when you would bark
When you finally did decide to sleep
Your paws covered your face and nose
You looked like a fluffy Angel laying there
Curled up with your eyes closed

For seven years you were my world
The apple of my eye
That kind of bond will never break
That's why it's hard to say goodbye
God help them up in heaven
If there's trouble, there you'll be
Wagging your tail and barking
While you wait for me

Better Off

I am better off alone
I am not happy here with you
Life's too short to be wasting time
This relationship is through

I deserve better than I've settled for
Surely there is more to life than this
The freedom to do whatever I want
To me that sounds like bliss

No more, where are you
What time will you be back
Compromising for the sake of compromise
I have had enough and that's a fact

Cooking meals and washing
No, I am not your bloody slave
That will be my epitaph
To sit above my grave

The kids are grown and here we are
Two strangers side by side
I am not staying in this loveless home
Just for the sake of pride

I can start again I have done it before
I will be happy and I will be free
There's nothing wrong with being on my own
In fact I will enjoy the company

I have packed my bags, keep the house
Goodbye to you, God bless
I wish you well but I am off you see
You can't put a price on happiness.

Butterfly

Living in the shadows
You have never seen the light
Too afraid to face the sun
The beams are far too bright

You have lived a half existence
At no time have you felt whole
Something is always missing
Never connecting with your soul

Your words they have no meaning
You don't speak from the heart
If asked to speak with feeling
You wouldn't know where to start

You have always been a slave in life
Trapped in your own cocoon
Your butterfly has never emerged
You're alive in your own tomb

How can you escape this fate
Unaware that it's not right
Wriggle and flap your wings a little
Then you might take flight

It's so easy to give good advice
From a place where I am free
I don't know what you've been through
As I call for you to join me

Just know you do have options
You don't ever have to be alone
Your choices determine the steps you take
Yet your journey is your own

Device

I am addicted to my phone
I cannot put the damn thing down
Flicking from app to app
To my device I know I'm bound
As soon as I wake, I reach for it
I have to know what's going on
Then waste hours and hours scrolling
This addiction really is that strong
I will not leave home without it
How an earth can I be reached
In fact, I cannot live without it

My phone has me under siege
I use it now for everything
From music to paying bills
I wish I could put it down just once
This addiction is making me ill
It's meant to make me feel connected
So why do I feel like I'm on my own
It has separated me from reality
I have never felt more alone
I don't have to talk anymore
It's so much easier just to text
If I don't get an instant response when typing
I'm left feeling angry and perplexed

My partner and I sit next to each other
Yet we couldn't be further apart
Both on our phones communicating
Silence has become an art
This is no longer sustainable
I need to formulate a plan
I want to break free from this monstrosity
Of having my phone glued to my hand

Choice

Where is the peace, don't I deserve any
Even when I sleep you wait in silence
So I must do battle as I rest with my eyes closed
It is so unfair I have been wronged
In both worlds by you and your cruelty
Your un-honest words, your persecution of me

I have had no justice, tried and convicted
By you and your followers, the irony
Without my say, without my day in court
Those that cast the first stone
You should have remained silent
Do I now stoop to your level, do I now retaliate
Where judging ears are present

Or do I rise above these waves of injustice
Hoping that the beams of truth will eventually shine
Then it dawns on me
The only voice that matters is the one that speaks the truth
My voice

It does not need to be wasted convincing fools
That have not the capacity or the bravery to speak for themselves
Think for themselves, too busy wanting to fit in
It must be so uncomfortable being a square peg in a round hole
If something is wrong and all agree with it, it is still wrong

I would rather row alone into a storm of truth knowing that it is the right
thing to do
In this life, it is your decision's, your choices that you must live with
I would rather live alone knowing I made the right choice, than sit within
a crowd knowing I had made the wrong one just to fit in.

Despair

I've hoovered the house is spotless
Cushions in their place
All the windows gleaming
In the reflection I see my face
Bruising on my eyes
The swelling can be seen
I know this nightmare that I'm living
Isn't just a dream

Everything he's hit me for
I've never done again
The next outburst is guaranteed
It's not if but when
I've cooked his favourite dinner
I've served it with a smile
If only I knew than what I know now
I would have run a mile

It is nearly bedtime
I've survived another day
Children sleeping in their beds
Now he'll want his way
The ordeal is finally over
He's snoring fast asleep
Tears rolling down my face
The future is so bleak

I can't tell friends or family
So scared of what he'll do
He'd kill me if I tried to run
I feel my life is through
One day I'll summon up the courage
I'll take the kids and run
When I'm feeling strong enough
Yet that day just hasn't come

Leap of Faith

Why is change so frightening
When you know it's for the best
What is it about pulling up those roots
That really gets you stressed

It just goes to show you
How comfortable you can be
Living within the darkest hole
Bright lights of freedom seems so scary

Changing an environment
To something you don't know
It's sometimes painful to be pushed
Out of your comfort zone

A new job, a new relationship
Perhaps a brand-new home
Facing your fear once and for all
Is something you should own

How do you think you got here
If it was not for your ability to grow
To spread your wings, take a leap of faith
You have more strength than you know

Be brave if you're not happy
You know what you must do
Take that step, make those changes
To do what's best for you.

Don't live where you're not comfortable
Just settling is such a waste
Do all you can to be happy and contented
Growth requires a little space

My Son

I'll never forget the day she told me
It came right out of the blue
The pregnancy test kit and a giggle
Telling me that we were having you

Two things happened over the next nine months
And I wanted you to know
Every day I dreamed of holding you
As I watched her belly grow

Before we knew it, there we were
In the maternity ward
Having you being handed to me
Being asked to cut the umbilical cord

Looking at your little face
Then hearing your first cry
I will love you and your mum with everything
Until the day I die

Seeing you being born my son
Words just can't describe
The love I felt made me well up
It was the best day of my life

I remember being told by your grandparents
He'll grow up so fast
I wish I could build a time machine son
So I could make these moments last

Everything I ever wanted
I got when I held you
My boy, my son your perfect
You are my dream come true.

Marriage

I never ever pictured this
Standing here with you
Having your hand in mine
While saying the words I do
When I saw you all those years ago
I thought this must be destiny
When I looked deep into your eyes
I knew you were the one for me
Now standing together in church
The bells are about to chime
We have finally exchanged our vows
I know that you're all mine

How beautiful you look my wife
Wearing that wedding ring
I get to spend my life with you
You are my everything
My face hurts from all the smiling
These are the happiest tears I've cried
I lifted your vail as I heard the words
You may now kiss your bride

In sickness and health, I will love you
By your side I will always be
I aim to be the perfect husband
For the perfect bride in front of me
I never ever thought about marriage
I wasn't sure if It was meant to be
You changed all of that forever
Unearthing the best version of me

We walk out to the organ playing
My heart bursting with pride
Family and friends, clapping and cheering
As we stood side by side
So we begin our married life
Having adventures like we planned
You then smiled and winked at me
Whispering my love is in safe hands.

Life Sentence

What an earth is happening
I seem to have lost a step
I'm slowing down, I don't know why
My tank has nothing left

Still hungry after eating
So tired after sleeping
I can't think on my feet anymore
Is my mind depleting

I get so very, very confused
With such simple things
Forgetting the names of the ones I love
Feeling the heartbreak that, that brings

I'm afraid to ask the question
To find out what is wrong
I might not want to hear the lyrics
To that sad, sad song

I fear the word dementia
An illness of the mind
The cruellest of all twists of fate
Why is life so unkind

This will impact everyone I love
We will all serve time
My friends and family are innocent
It's this disease that it is the crime

Taking everything that I am
Everything that makes me, me
Until all that's left is an empty shell
Of the man I used to be

The ones I love will have no choice
There is nothing they can do
So for however long I am able
Hear me when I say that I love you.

Second Chances

What is it with second chances
You weren't worthy of the first
To think I would ever take you back
I'm afraid that bubbles burst

You never did deserve my heart
But I gave it all the same
No more handouts of my love
You've lost your ticket to that train

The lies with along with all your tears
All a part of your wonderful act
Now I know how that movie goes
I want my money back

So glad that your mask slipped
Giving me a glimpse of the real you
Showing me what I had in store
I am so relieved now we're through

My love and time I wasted
Everything I gave, you took it all
You just did what all players do
You got cocky and dropped the ball

What I am you do not deserve
It can be painful to hear the truth
I will no longer lay in your bed of lies
I must protect myself from you

On my way to better times
Healing slowly day by day
I deserve love from a man of his word
Not a player that wants to play

Healed

I am a drop of water in the aether
Just one grain of sand
A pebble on the ocean floor
Yet I know who I am

The arms you need around you
The smile that lifts your soul
The tissue for the tears you cry
The piece that makes you whole

My being here is justified
By the good I feel in you
My time is never wasted
Watching you unearth the truth

May our journey be a long one
Listen with your heart as I confide
To get to where you need to be in life
You will have me by your side

Remembering our first encounter
After what you had been through
I introduced you to your courage
That fire still burns inside of you

How did you discover your strength
Your fate was never sealed
What you needed you've always had
And that is why you healed.

Unfrequented Love

From afar I have loved you
From here I have been able to see
How beautiful you are, so kind and caring
For us it was never meant to be
So I have loved you from a distance
Hoping all your dreams come true
For you to be happy and healthy
Finding someone that's worthy of you
From here my heart's protected
This is as close as I come
I couldn't put myself through the thought of losing you
Feeling like I'd been burned by the sun
So from afar I will love you
That's okay I'll take it, it's fine
Learning to except I can love but not have you
And that you will never be mine.

Broken Angel

Why don't you see what I see
Your beauty is beyond compare
A gentle soul, kind and loving
Yet life has been so unfair
The mirror you use is broken
Words of kindness you just cannot hear
You feel that love never chose you
Your heart has been flooded with tears
Your confidence is shattered
Your self-esteem has gone
Wondering how it ever got to this
Your life's like a sad love song
The precipice approaches
The time for change has come
Be kind in the way that you treat yourself
You are a star so shine like one.

I Drank You In

I drank you in
All of you
The parts of you
You never knew
Your beautiful way
The kindest smile
Your way of being
Your sense of style
Your eyes of love
Your body of care

I really felt you
I felt you there
I held your hand
But we didn't touch
We held each other
That meant so much
We were connected
Two became one
Sitting in silence
Warmed by each other's sun
Thank you for sharing

For just being you
You're so amazing
In all that you do
You breathed me in
I breathed you out
That's what this experience
Is all about
I loved you
And you loved me
I will remember this moment
For eternity.

Self-harm

Another cut
Where you cannot see
When I am angry
I lash out privately
The sting, the pain
Doesn't last that long
The lacerations and bruising
In a week they're gone
I get so frustrated
It's bad for my health
It's the only way I cope
When I'm harming myself

If I could just talk
To explain this is real
I would just get shut down
You don't understand how I feel
This all started at home
Although it sounds absurd
I remained silence
I couldn't utter a word

All of my trauma
Is buried within
The way I release it
Is through cutting my skin
I cannot talk about it
I don't have the words
If I did talk about it
Would I even be heard
I want my anger to end
I would love to feel calm
Being at peace in my body
Then I wouldn't self-harm.

Lost Child

I couldn't find my inner child
I called but he never came
Perhaps if we had a better time back then
He would show his face again
I called and called, I lost my voice
Broken I couldn't cope
I felt so lonely, so heartbroken
I had given up all hope
A reassuring voice I heard
Said I've never left your side
To be where you are today
Fills me with so much pride
I turned to look and there I was
The child from so long ago
He said the time for sadness has passed my friend
I love you more than you will ever know.

Regret

You have to let it go once and for all
I can see what you think I can't see
This guilt you carry, your full of regret
Yes it's that obvious to me
I can see the pain you are hiding
You can't disguise what is on show
There's no malice you followed your heart
It's time to let it go

The decisions, were done with the best of intentions
Staying, would of made things far worse
You did what was right for all parties involved
For once you have put yourself first
I have watched you carry this guilt
A heavy burden you've dragged around
The time has come for forgiveness
Put those unwanted feelings down
You shouldn't continue to punish yourself
The healing is ready to start
Take the reins, head towards contentment
There is no crime in following your heart.

Perspectives

I never meant to hurt you but because of the rift between us
I just floated further and further away, calling out but you couldn't hear
me, I couldn't hear myself. My kindness and love being drowned out by
my own anger and hurt, holding me deep under water until the need to
connect was lost.

It is the child in me that never gives up hope, he spoke without success,
you couldn't translate, or understand the language.
That is why the attempts to make amends seemed so ungenuine
they seemed childish, they are. The adult is not the one reaching out,
my adult is still very angry with you. It's the child, my inner child, that
wants to be friends again.

It just takes a little while longer to bridge the divide because it's from my
inner child's perspective. He wants to put the fractured pieces back
together, he wants to initiate the repair. It's only when you're willing to
listen with patient ears and an understanding heart to all parties, the rift
can be healed between us all.

Red Flags

Have you ever stayed in a relationship
Just to prove the doubters wrong
You knew in your heart it was over
That the love had gone
You ignored your friend's advice
They say that love is blind
Common sense told you to move on out
Stubbornness made you stay behind
So red flags were collected
You forgave them time after time
Under the illusion that they would change
And in the end, you'd be fine
In silence your heart asked a question
Why are we putting up with this
Surely we would be better off alone
Too late to contemplate the what's and if's
What are the doubters going to say
The ones telling you from the start
Avoid this one like the plague, they said
Or you'll suffer along with your heart
Common sense then steps in
We are swimming in quicksand
This relationship is dead in the water
Now please just take my hand
Common sense and my heart
Came to my rescue
They saved me from this living nightmare
Yours could do the same for you
The only voice that ever matters
Is yours and yours alone
Heed red flags and warning signs
For a happy peaceful home
Give yourself some space to heal,
Time for your heart to clean up the mess
Then and only then in time
Will you be able to receive real happiness
A troubled relationship is not a waste
With hurtful knowledge you have earned
It's experience that money can't buy
If you heed the lessons learned.

Dad

I can see you are upset my son
That I have caused that pain
Let's take a breath and talk it out
Without anger or any blame
No matter whatever happens
You will always be my boy
You are the apple of my eye
Filling me with love and joy

I know you can be stubborn
You get that trait from me
Like me when the red mist descends
You can't think with clarity
I know you have been struggling
A weight you've carried feeling so alone
I am always here for you my son
Don't face those demons on your own

It's me that should of reached out
I could hear it in your voice
You took on far too much my boy
Not feeling like you had a choice
I am so very proud of you
The man that you've become
You are the greatest thing I ever did
I'm blessed to have you as my son

We can work this issue out
Emotions will settle in time you'll see
No matter what I will always love you
You are the greatest part of me
Alas these words were never spoken
I wished you'd wrote this poem Dad
Not only have I lost my father
I've lost the best friend I've ever had.

Leopards

Is this what it's come to
Now you've got to write to me
Many times we've been through this
You've got to set him free
Choose your words very carefully
When you decide to jot them down
So when you read them back out loud
The reasons will be found
You are not a sex toy
To be used then cast aside

Promises of a love so meaningful
Was the bate he filled with lies
He hasn't made you feel worthless
You have done that on your own
Losing your sense of self-worth my love
Even with him you're so alone
No it is not raining
Your tears warm your cheeks
Putting up with this for far too long
I don't even need to speak
It's you that's let this happen
Again, and again and again

There's a reason Leopards have their spots
It's you who needs to change
You are so, so beautiful
With a kind and gentle soul
You have the strength if needed
Deserving the earth if, truth be told
When you have moments of weakness
Read this poem written just for you
Sit down and take a deep breath
Then you'll know what to do
You don't need him to feel loved
Inner strength will get you through
When the universe is ready
What's meant, will come to you.

Little Boy

A childhood filled with trauma
He knew nothing else
Too young to talk and process
So he kept it to himself
Innocent and defenceless
A child that needed care
Through teary eyes he looked at them
Thinking this is so unfair
What was their duty as his parents
Protect with love, so he believed
Yet time and time and time again
He was neglected and deceived
He did not ask to be their son
He did not have a choice
So young and so defenceless
He hadn't found his voice
The abuse he received has scarred him
The little boy that lived in shame
With a mum incapable of mothering
They were both to blame
Why did his Father never speak up
His silence felt like a crime
He was just as culpable
For that the boy served time
He couldn't wait to breakout
So he allowed himself to dream
To escape this life of misery
As soon as he had turned sixteen
What power he had at that age
Facing the world all on his own
Saving himself from this nightmare
That place was never home
That little boy became a man
He grew up with me
When I look deep into his eyes
His strength is what I see
I will love and protect him
Give the support he needs
I am so very, very proud of him
Because that little boy is me.

Tina

How does it make you feel
Knowing I'm your only son
Wanting nothing from you
I will never call you mum

You blew your chance forever
When you discarded me
I had to step back from it all
To gain some clarity

I did not see it at first
Thinking I'd done something wrong
I thought that's why you left us
That is why you'd gone

Hard to grasp at four years of age
I can't believe I was that young
Have you got any idea at all
Of the damage you have done

Attachment disorder
Abandonment fear
You did not want me
It was so obviously clear

I tried to connect
Again, and again
To be rejected by you
Burdened with shame

The last time I saw you
I was just seventeen
Still longing for a mother
Who's actions she'd want to redeem
That was never you
Always thinking of yourself
Selfish and self-centred
Only interested in wealth

Never having children of my own
For years I struggled to settle down

I always left girlfriends first
Believing they wouldn't stick around

Over thirty years and counting
I've finally let go of my shame
If I ever have to talk about you, Tina
I use your Christian name.

Big Boys Don't Cry

Why is it deemed weak
For a man to cry
To show real emotion
Revealing a vulnerable side

Men should express their feelings
Without persecution or fear
Having an emotional outlet
Making thoughts and feelings clear

It starts with the man as a child
Big boys are not meant to cry
Without any explanation given
The boy has no idea why

The next time he is hurting
He will lock it all away
He won't articulate what's going on
Learning there's nothing to say

Once the boy becomes a man
The damage is permanently done
He won't communicate his feelings
To me, you, or any one

This is such a vicious cycle
That we must work to break
Teaching boys to talk about feeling
Then a more complete man will we make.

Am I Crazy

Facing the traffic head on
In this world without a care
Happy for this day to be my last
Even my fear is scared

I don't ever think like you do
I can't see what it is you see
Black and white with a little grey
And that's fine by me

Depression is my playground
Loneliness is my best friend
Anxiety is oh so reliable
What I have's the perfect blend

You don't know what's going on
We keep that to ourselves
We don't talk to strangers
That could be bad for our ill health

My business doesn't need your nose
Neither do my affairs
Thinking the words, are you okay
Are some sign you actually care

I must straighten up my jacket
The buckles dig in if their too tight
Better for all concerned I stay in
There's a full moon out tonight

So tell me am I crazy Doc
My prognosis had been left to you
It takes one to know one apparently
So are you a little crazy too

Procrastinating

I've got so much to do
I haven't a clue where to start
I've been Procrastinating
Mastering the art
I let it all build up
Intentions were honestly good
I will start it all tomorrow
Then don't when I know I should
Whether it be clutter
The house is such a mess

Where do I begin I wonder
I don't know what to address
Is it my anxiety
It's on one today
I am going to sort my life out
As soon as it goes away
Then there's the headaches
Something's got to give
I have problems I can't face
I am losing the will to live
I will ask for some help
I must, my future's bleak

When I get around to it of course
I'll call the doctor sometime next week
The weeks become months
The months become years
I've buried my head in the sand
I can't face my own fears
I know I seem distant
I haven't been myself
Forgetting what myself looks like
Believe me I need your help

My Definition

What is it that makes being in love so special, the feelings you have, the look you give each other when you are together, meaning a million things. The butterflies when you think about them when
they are not with you. The warm feeling in your soul when they step softly across your mind, when you look across a crowded room and your eyes meet, everyone else disappears, leaving the two of you in a cloud of love and contentment.

When you want to show them off to the world yet your conflicted with the fact that you don't want to share them with anyone.
That you can close your eyes and watch the first time you met each other a thousand times over and still never get tired of the replay.
That every love song is written about the two of you, describing your every emotion. That you sing for no reason at all, feeling warm on the coldest of days as you feel them swimming in your soul.

You could listen to them talk from sundown until sunrise and not feel tired but energised like your heart has been nourished with words they've spoken, each syllable has landed ever so softly on your ears. You could never imagine them not in your life, the thought would be too painful to bare, you would not function, you would not be able to sleep and life would never be the same again.

The thought of planning a future does not need any more detail than you'll be together. Your cheeks go red when anyone mentions their name to you, like a silly school kid being teased.

You experience feelings you have never felt before, they are overwhelming, frightening but also exciting and exhilarating. When you daydream, your heart can race while you are laying down thinking about them, you would climb a mountain to meet them at the top to say hello.

You would do anything for one another and nothing would be too much to put a smile on their face and hear laughter from their lips. You would have each other's backs no matter the odds, you against the world if necessary.

In your eyes they are perfect, even the imperfections are beautiful, You can picture yourselves together until the end of time. Until the light of the universe goes out and even then, even in the darkness you will be whole. You have all you have ever wanted with you for an eternity. Holding and nourish your very being, when I think about love, this is what I imagine it to be.

Lost Thoughts

It is ok to be sad
It is ok to feel lost
It is ok to carry a broken heart
As long as you are the one that holds it
It is you who will understand
It is you that will have the chance to repair it
The time you need to collect lost thoughts
The time to hold your sadness close
Your love will charge no cost
This is the way of things
Be mindful of your emotions
Of how you really feel inside
Be true to yourself
Be patient and gentle with your feelings
Those broken pieces of your heart
Can be whole again
It will just take time to heal.

First Crush

That feeling that wanting
I remember my first crush
Ireland the summer of 88
When I first fell in love

Something changed when I saw her
An emotion I cannot describe
Just being in her company
Made me come alive

When I looked into her eyes
She looked into mine
Like a thunderstorm, lightning struck
A moment frozen in time

I never even kissed her
We didn't hold each other's hands
Yet I was having feelings
That I could not understand

Although it was a lifetime ago
I drift off thinking of her for a while
Those big green Irish eyes
Her beautiful country smile

We were young and innocent
Those experiences were all brand new
Our whole lives ahead of us
I pictured spending mine with you

That summer of love was beautiful
Able to set loving feelings free
Such a shame I went back to England
I guess it was never meant to be.

It's Not Fine

Someone upset me today
I said it's okay, no it's fine
It wasn't their feelings being hurt
As usual those feelings were mine

In the past I wonder when I did this
If I was made to see
That no it's not fine and not okay
How that would of impacted me

Talking without thinking
Untold damage can be caused
Before I talk, I think first
Sometimes it's good to pause

If I am now made to feel like this
When I'm about to say it's fine
I know I deserve much better
So, when you're talking, please be kind.

Teenager

I'm so bloody uncomfortable
I never ever fit in
No friends, no one to talk to
So unhappy beneath the skin
I don't want to talk, I'm never friendly
How can I be, I don't have friends
Not into what people my age are into
That's where conversations end

Indoors things are much easier
Outside I feel impending doom
At home I don't interact
I just hide away in my room
Social media isn't social
Even there I feel alone
Although it brings me no joy at all
I'm constantly glued to the phone

It's hard and I'm just a teenager
Is this what life's meant to be about
If it is I know I can't take anymore
Thinking I'll take the easy way out
I read about teenager's suicide rates
The statistics, why they're so high
Permanently impacting those left behind
Left broken with no idea why

If I could talk and be heard
If someone out there could relate
I'd better understand what's going on
And why I struggle to communicate.

Sergeant

I wonder what he dreams about
When he's fast asleep
His little legs are running
While he's tucked up next to me

Is he chasing the neighbour's cat
Maybe he's playing with his ball
Perhaps he's barking at the postman
Who's made an unexpected call

He whimpers quietly growling
Paws twitching and legs kicking out
I gently stroke and reassure him
There's nothing to worry about

My English bull terrier, Sergeant
He is a rescue dog you see
It's actually quite ironic
He really rescued me

He has been a livewire
Since the day I picked him up
As soon as I laid eyes on him
I instantly fell in love

Bull terriers do love zooming
Spinning around and around
They also can't help creeping
Tiptoeing without making a sound

You can tell when he's up to mischief
If he's silent and out of sight
I can't be mad at him for long though
My fluffy white and brown delight

Man's best friend, he's so much more
My boy who loves unconditionally
More than I ever could've wished for
Sargent means the absolute world to me

Ruby

My baby girl, a golden Princess
She is such a beautiful pooch
Dog De Bordeaux, the name of her breed
The one from Turner and Hooch

I picked her up from a stranger
She wasn't wanted anymore
On April the 1st, 2016
I had no idea what was in store

I think we were kindred spirits
Abandoned without an explanation why
It took her six months to build up some trust
Now she won't leave my side

When I got her, she was in season
I really hadn't thought this thing through
I took her home and Sargent saw her
He thought his dreams had come true

My English Bull Terrier fell in love instantly
It really was love at first sight
Trying to impress her for seven years straight
Showing off, morning, noon and night

She might not come when you call her
When she sleeps, she takes up the bed
If she hears a crisp packet rattling
She's looking at you, tilting her head

I cannot imagine life without her
Such a gentle, unique, loving personality
Ruby has changed my life for the better
Forever, one of the family.

Arcade

Another pound
Click press play
I have been in here
Most of the day

The arcade
It's my second home
I am up at the moment
I'm in the zone

A couple of bars,
I just need two more
Let me just quickly
Change up a score

I need to win back
All the money I've lost
I don't want to contemplate
What it has cost

My money is gone
I have spent all my wages
It's start of the month
I'm so bloody frustrated

I can't believe what I've done
I say never again
My gambling addiction
Has caused nothing but pain

With my life
I'm playing Russian roulette
I've spent all my money
I have got nothing left

I'll never learn
I'll never change
No amount, of good, advice
Can separate me from my vice

One more pound one more spin

My luck will change, I am due a win
Once again, all is lost
My house, my wife and kids the cost

Good advice, wasn't good for me
I didn't want to stop you see
I broke all promises that I made
To spend my money in the arcade

Next month I'll pay these debts back
It is time to get my life back on track
Who am I kidding I won't ever change
Here is a twenty-pound note
Can I have some change?

A Pint or Two

I haven't got a problem
I have it under control
I can stop whenever I want
No, it's not taking its toll
I'm just out socialising
With my friends from the pub
Oh what does she want now
Please stop texting me love
I will be home when I'm home
I fancy another pint or two
I will drink what I want when I want
What's it got to do with you

I used to be such a lightweight
I could get drunk on a score
Now I can drink pint after pint
With no effect anymore
She's always moaning
I can't seem to do anything right
She will have to bath the kids
Read the bedtime story tonight
I can't handle the nagging
That is all she ever does
Hard to believe it really
We were once madly in love

Now I drink at home
It helps me relieve my stresses
Who does she think she is talking to
Calling me a drunken old mess
I have been fired from work
I didn't kick up a fuss
Grassed up for drinking on the job
I hated driving that bus
She wants me out of our house
It's not good for the kids
She doesn't seem to care about me
I've now got nowhere to live

I'm not allowed to see the children
She's changed all the locks

If I turn up unannounced
She said she'll call the cops
I have nothing now
No wife, kids, job or home
Just this horrible addiction
I can't face on my own
I want to turn this around
Clean up, find a place to stay
Kick this habit once and for all
With the help of AA.

Apology

A genuine apology
Sincere and to be believed
Once given and accepted
Friendships can be achieved
Never refuse an apology
You don't know what it's been through
It's journey may have been difficult
As it found its way to you
Take this sorry as a gift
A present on Christmas Day
Be kind and show forgiveness
You don't know how hard it was to say
Your load will feel a little lighter
Believe me, you will see
You'd be amazed at the powers
Of a genuine apology.

Addictions

When we as children face trauma
We self-soothe to ease the pain
Which can transform into addiction
Suffering burdened with shame
Addiction can take many forms
They're cunning and very sly
Those that set this wheel in motion
Point fingers asking questions why
Whether we drown in alcohol
So we can numb the pain
Sending wolves to erase memories
So we don't feel worthless again

The syringe and the needle
Our poison isn't chosen carefully
Spiralling completely out of control
The addiction is all people see
Stealing from the ones we love
Lying right into their faces
Then we're judged for surface drama
That judgement is very misplaced
Looking then walking right past me
Like I was not even there
Can you not see that I'm suffering
I feel invisible, why don't you care

Am I not worth a second chance
How would you treat me if I was a child
That's where it all started for me
I wasn't born angry and wild
The way I behave, it's a defence mechanism
I was not always like this you see
You'd know the truth if you knew my story
Taking time to get to know me

Do not judge those you don't know
Kindness is the only projection to send
You have no idea how I have suffered
My truth you could not comprehend
Just being there to hear me talk
Could kick start my recovery

We all have stories that need to be told
Please take some time to listen to me
Momentous events have devastating consequences
If you see the signs, you might understand
It takes a special person to be non-judgmental
Start healing by just holding my hand.

My Darkness

Can you hold my hand
would that be okay
I need some reassurance
Something more than words can say

Lately I haven't been myself
Too busy pleasing others
Feeling empty and neglected
My vulnerability now uncovered

I found a calmness in your eyes
Honesty in your smile
Peace, as we sat in silence
I haven't felt that in a while

All I am is what I offer
I want nothing more than you
Can I dare to dream out loud
That you want that too

I found you in my darkness
You made your way to me
I've realised I don't need light
To be able to really see

The door to me is open
If you want it here's the key
Welcomed with open arms forever
What will be will always be

Heartbreaker

I shouldn't have to make you love me
I can't teach a blind man to see
Saying I was everything you ever wanted
That was just a fallacy
I gave in to all your desires
I was all in, right from the start
I gave you everything I had and more
I gave you the key to my heart
Never have I felt so happy
Or wanted somebody so much
This started with a look and a smile
You were a lifelong crush

I showed you off to the world
My parents even called you their son
Not only have you betrayed me
You have betrayed everyone
Thinking my friends were happy for us
Seeing my dreams had come true
That is why I guess love is blind
I couldn't see one of them wanted you
Where am I meant to go now
What an earth am I meant to do
Apologies are all meaningless
I'm never going to forgive you

Building my whole world around you
Wanting marriage and a family
I'm not interested in your empty words
Or half-hearted apologies
It's not you that's got to face the music
It's me that has it all to do
Every time I'm asked what happened
I'll end up crying again over you
Will I ever get over the heartbreak
Will my heart ever mend
Love stories are adult fairy tales
Your affair brought mine to an end.

Kiss You

I think about you constantly
You are imprinted on my mind
What would it be like to kiss your lips
To feel them pressed to mine

I've thought of how your kiss would taste
Would it leave me wanting more
Would my imagination then run riot
Thinking of what could be in store

I am going to have to sit on this
Not wanting to confront this ongoing issue
I'm not in a position to take this further
Even though I want to kiss you

I cannot risk this being bad timing
Or some cruel twist of fate
It would really hurt if you said to me
I'm not someone that you'd want to date

I have decided for once to stay silent
My true feelings I'll have to hide
I couldn't take being rejected by you
I shall protect my delicate pride

I will leave it to my imagination
A dream that won't ever come true
Accepting it's as close as I'll get
And friendship's the best I can do.

Feeling Depressed

Don't worry I'll do it tomorrow
I cannot be arsed today
I know I said I'd do it last week
But things just got in the way
I am not feeling motivated
I'm really not in the mood
For God's sake stop going on
It is your fault, I'm being rude
Jesus will you stop nagging
If I said I'll do it, then I will

It's your fault I'm feeling depressed
It's you who's making me ill
I can't understand, I feel so lethargic
I just haven't got any drive
Sometimes I have the darkest thoughts
Not appreciating what's good in my life
I don't want to get medicated
I can't beat depression on my own
I'm not strong enough to reach out for help
It's why I feel so alone
Yes I hear what you're saying
You're right I understand, I see
You can get the help that I you need
Says the man looking in the mirror at me.

Herding Cats

I cannot put it back in the box
This feeling I have for you
It would be as hard as herding cats
Which is impossible to do

Where did these emotions come from
I have never felt this way before
This feeling I have of excitement
Is something I want to explore

The feeling, it is a wanting
I really don't know what to do
I don't want to put it back in the box
I want to be connected to you

My mind is in total freefall
Yet I am not afraid you see
For some reason when I pull the cord
I know that you'll be next to me

Maybe this is kismet
Something written in the stars
The magic encapsulating your being
That makes you who you are

A real friendship can be priceless
Maybe this is what this will be
I've learned you just can't herd cats
So I'll just wait and see.

I Want Out

I want to get out of here
When's my sentence up
This feels so unfair to me
You can't even call it bad luck
You know I've been a good boy
That should knock a few years off
I am fed up with being pulled about
That's it, I've had enough
If only I wasn't so frail
I used to be made of sterner stuff
Their once was a time you know
I was considered quite tough

I'm not eating this tripe anymore
Where's my full English fry up
Told when I can drink and eat
The only thing that's mine is my cup
Stuck here with the same bloody view
Waiting for days, for a visit from you
I see the guards have let you in
You can't trust them you know
They will soon change their tune
The minute you walk out the door
Did you remember to sign in then
Like they told you to do
If you don't book in first
They'll make it awkward for you

Not allowed to watch programmes
They say I stay up too late
I have had enough of this shite
Having much more than I can take
I have got no privacy
They come in whenever they choose
They pull me about all of the time
Even when I'm on the loo
Feeding me horrible tablets
While I sit with strangers
I am a gentleman you know
I don't condone this behaviour
Constantly surrounded

But I feel so alone
Please get me out of here
I desperately want to go home
Let me make a quick call
Please give me my phone
How long must I wait I wonder
To escape this bloody care home.

If Nothing Changes

I dare not let them know at work
How I really feel
I am really struggling
My mental health issues are real

I feel I will be laughed at
Ridiculed by my peers
So I make out I'm alright
They all have no idea

I smile when I feel like I'm dying
I laugh when I want to cry
I cannot sustain this facade anymore
Holding tears that fill my eyes

I am not sure it's safe to reach out
Or in what direction I should go
I wish I could put my trust out there
Then my true feelings I could show

Nothing changes if nothing changes
I'm at breaking point it's so hard
Tomorrow I am going to take that step
Making an appointment with HR.

First Session

Can you hear me
Hear me clearly
Really, honestly, truthfully
Sincerely

I have been dreading this
Resisting it, having a hissy fit
Really wanting no part of it

I have been dreading today
Not knowing what I'm meant to say
I'm not going to open up
I'm not built that way

I have been referred
It has been advised
Some counselling is required
I'm not sure if that's wise

Here I am, with all to bare
Sitting in your counselling chair
I am so nervous, anxious
I can hardly breathe
I'd do anything to leave

But here I sit, frozen
It's not the route, I would've chosen
How are you going to help me
Tell me, can you heal me

How does this work
Can you make me see
Can you set my anxiety free
Is it left to me to do the talking
God I really feel like walking

But if I do nothing changes
Instead of feeling trapped
I want my issues trapped in cages

Well, I have come this far

Might as well give it a go, you never know
If I leave, I have nothing to show

For being brave, facing fear
What's the worst that could happen here
You seem friendly and welcoming too
After everything that I've been through

It's not questions and answers, it's not a quiz
I'm going to trust my gut, hello my name is…

A Smile Without Advice

Listening is so simple
A skill that is a gift
Just to be and listen
Can give the perfect lift
No words by you are needed

Be kind and make that clear
Fill the space and sit back
So you can really hear
Silence without agenda
A smile without advice
Listen without prejudice

So words aren't spoken twice
If you have never felt heard
Some have ignored you and your soul
Feeling your words are worthless
Can really take its toll

Counselling must be meticulous
Heart and mind in the right place
Listening such an underrated art
Along with providing a safe space
So be silent, tuned in and ready
Quiet, present and grounded
Allow your body language to speak
Then outcomes can be astounding.

The Web

I hear it all the time why can't liars just tell the truth, why didn't they tell me they just wanted a plaything, if they did, they wouldn't be able to get inside your emotional front door. You would never let them in so, you hear the most beautiful lies that soften you.

The bricks of that wall of yours are removed ever so gently before you even know where you are. You're exposed, vulnerable and those very well protected feelings of wanting the love of the deepest kind, you had encased for so long are now worn firmly on your sleeve.

Where the beams of a lying son can burn them, you feel such a fool you should have known better, your closest allies warned you.
Why didn't you listen, maybe because the spider made that web so comfortable with the strand of each lie weaved, that is when you finally hear the dinner bell ringing.

You are the main course in this web of deceit but by eventually breaking free, you lose some of yourself. Left behind stuck on that web you escaped from, instead of feeling elation that you are finally free you feel your heart being crushed.

As you firmly squeeze it back inside that wall of safety you created it hurts so much more because your heart is a lot bigger now than when it was exposed so long ago

That is why the pain is constant, why the kick in your gut that winded you so heavily will not dissipate. You despair, don't, you feel worthless, don't. Leave the liar to swim in those emotions, imagine them struggling to stay afloat.

There hasn't been a number written that can match your values infinite, you can start there as you recover, leave the liar out deep in the storm as you're able to row yourself safely back to shore.
Be thankful you are back on land, steadfast on the island of truth where liars are not allowed to trespass.

Hello

I have travelled so far just to be here
My feet ache my shoes are worn
This journey has taken me all of my life
It began once I was born

Destiny or maybe providence
I wonder if choice had a role to play
The universe and perhaps a little faith
Brought us together today

Who I am, is what I've experienced
Every step I've taken you cannot see
My journey is not my story
So when I speak, please listen to me

It's hard to hear if you have an opinion
It's hard to see when you've already judged
I want nothing from you that you cannot afford
Patients and unconditional love

Our journey's do not define us
As we share this humble abode
Let's begin this new chapter together
And start it by saying hello.

Divorce

How has it come to this
You said till death do us part
Not only are you leaving me
You're also breaking my heart
You were the love of my life
And my best friend too
Now you can't even talk to me
Except to say that we're through
I loved you more than anyone
I loved you more than everyone

I put everything into our marriage
Now you tell me you are done
How can you be so cold
Saying the relationships run its course
I never thought I'd hear those words
Telling me you want a divorce
Have you found someone else
Did you ever really care
I deserve some answers
I'm not going anywhere

If you really want to leave
You can take your stuff and go
Don't even think about taking the kids
Do they even know
I can't believe how much you've changed
I don't know who you are
Best friends and lovers to strangers again
I can't believe it's gone this far
Hearing you say you don't want to talk
Or see me ever again

That you don't love me anymore
It's so heart breaking
I am devastated and empty
I don't know what to do
I don't know if I'll ever recover
How I'm I meant to get over you.

Support

I wanted to reach out to you
I didn't want you suffering today
Wanting you to know I was thinking of you
To make sure you're okay
It's okay to not be okay
It's okay to be heartbroken too
Being sad is a natural response
To everything that's happened to you
Times have been extremely tough
Situations, horrendously painful
Not wanting to hear it'll be okay
It's condescending and extremely distasteful

No one understands what you're going through
I get it, you think I have no idea
I don't but I just want you to know
If and when you need me, I will be here
I'm not one to compare feelings
Just to have a connection with you
I'm here so you don't suffer alone
After everything you've been through

If you want to sit in silence you can
Small talk is not necessary for me
Just send a text, call or email
When you feel ready for company
Real support doesn't need a label
I've got you if you breakdown and cry
I will hold you until you can hold yourself
I won't need an explanation why
Sometimes words aren't needed
In action is where the proof will be
No matter the time or place I'll be there
You can always rely on me.

Depression

Depression a sentence you never went to court for,
you cannot even remember the crime you committed.
Here you are in solitary confinement, trapped, darkness
and solitude are your only comfort.

You do not know how much time you have left on your sentence,
every minute feels like an hour and every hour feels like a year.
You are uncomfortable in your own skin, like a suit that does not fit.
It is tight and it digs into you, it is not your style. Not only do you look
uncomfortable, you feel uncomfortable to.

You feel like the prison that holds you is in a country where you do not
speak the language, you cannot understand visitors or the inmates. You
cannot communicate your feelings and be understood. Frustration takes
hold like a tick on the skin that cannot be removed without risk of
infection. Here you are without the ability to connect with anyone, in a
place you cannot describe, with a condition that cannot be diagnosed.

"Can't you hear me, I'm suffering; can't you see me, I'm right here!"
Depression does not allow you to communicate in this way.
It whispers so others cannot hear, taking you off to be alone and
isolated. The roots can take hold and bury themselves deep.
So clever to be unseen to the untrained eye. I can see, I can see the
roots and feel your suffering, as it pours out of you silently.

You do speak a language that I understand, I have the language to help
you understand it too, it's okay to not be okay, without having to hide in
the dark all alone. All you need to do is reach out when you can and I
will find you, the you that is buried, the you that you thought was lost
forever.

We can take each other's hands and together find the way back to you,
you that is happy in darkness or light. The you that is confident in
silence or conversation. The roots of depression will no longer be able
to take a hold when you are again at your most vulnerable point. I am
every counsellor worth their salt if you do not believe me just reach out
and see.

Four Seasons

Such a lovely time to be had at winter making snowmen, snowball fights, open fires, wrapping presents, putting up a christmas tree. Sitting together around the table for christmas dinner singing and laughing, renewing friendships, sharing old stories. The best part of the winter season is seeing in the new year with the ones you love.

The new year, then spring, puts a spring into your step as the green shoots first appear. The flowers start to grow, it gets a little lighter in the mornings. New life begins as the chick's hatch, their mothers tweet familiar songs at the breaking of the dawn.

The summertime, ice cream vans, sunshine, suntan cream, sunburn, water fights, buckets and spades. Toes buried deep in the sand on a beautiful beach somewhere, the time to fly off to another country drawing every closer. Living out that dream holiday a year ago you'd planned.

Autumn time, we wave goodbye to the summer, watching the colours change on the leaves from green to red then yellow and finally brown as they fall. Our feet wet from the due on the grass as the sun rises In the morning over your garden. You can see a spider waiting in a perfect web she's weaved. The kids are all now back in school, play grounds full of noise at lunchtime. It's starting to get a little colder jumpers and coats back on show. Before you know it, it's Halloween

Not long now until christmas approaches again, this is the way of life. How time flies, the week becomes a month in a flash, January becomes December in the blink of an eye. Take the time to appreciate and embrace all of the seasons as you pass them throughout the year.

Search Party

There are truths I don't want to hear
Realities I don't want to face
Some will be far too painful for me
Making the world a lonelier place
Ambling and stumbling throughout life
Sinking slowly in a deluge of quicksand
What I imagined in this life for myself
The reality is not what I'd planned
How can I ever be reached
I haven't even sent up a flare
No search party is looking for me
No one is even aware
Isolated I am all on my own
My world such a crowded place
A deafening noise in solitude
Screaming I have no time to waste
The truth is you're not here anymore
A reality I've been forced to embrace
Painfully having no choice but to except it
That's where my belief has been placed.

The Shell

You can only be who you are
You cannot be anyone else
You will find they are already taken
The substance that covers your bones
Love, embrace and cherish it
For it holds you all together
The skin you are wrapped in
Your perfect birth, day, gift
Rejoice in the colours chosen
You are packed into that matter that retains you
Your very being
The flesh, bone, spirit, that encapsulates you
Unique to the last detail, your remarkable
It's only your shell that we are touching on
All the paper in the world wouldn't be enough
To start the first chapter to the depth of you
For that is another story entirely, that only you can write.

Complete Control

Each of us has our own story to tell
We have all been broken in our own way
Uniquely damaged by the journeys we have taken
Whether of our choosing or otherwise
All impacted by different bumps in the road
That have left different types of bruising and scars for each of us
Some we heal from, and others leave a permanent reminder of events
past

Unfortunately, the earliest chain of events we had no control over
We weren't driving
Just passengers, as so we saw a lot more
Effected deeply, taking in the unpleasant views and experiences
Whether our eyes were open or closed, conscious or unconscious
Memories embedded forever into the neocortex
Poisonous seeds planted so deeply they can't be picked out by hand
they have to grow and flourish

Then perhaps in later years they can be pulled out, stem to root
If we are able to grow and develop, we get to sit in the driver's seat,
Do not be fooled we are never in complete control
Metaphorically, we still have to follow the road markings
Governed by the laws of the road
Where are you going to drive now you have the wheel
What sights are you going to see
How about the roads and streets that are familiar
Better the devil you know

If we had a map, if we knew where we were going to end up
Then perhaps we would take the easiest route
The most beautiful views, accompanied by the most pleasant sounds
Avoiding past turmoil and trauma to a destination of peace and
contentment
But we don't, we never will, that's precious information never to be
attained
So, we pass familiar streets of torment and trauma, houses of the most
awful memories
Sometimes stopping, visiting as a long-lost friend or the most
unwelcome guest

How does the healing occur

How do we reach a destination of contentment and inner peace
Is it by asking the way, or following our intuition
Those with real experience know the way
Having a deeper understanding of what impact personal trauma has
There awareness comes from their own personal perspective
You are given the safest directions only by those that have that understanding
Others may direct you to the right destination with good intentions
Only via the most painful route
As they have no semblance of you or your very unique journey already travelled
I don't have the answers for I am on my own journey
If I get lost along the way, please be kind if I ask you for directions

Reach Out

I am a Counsellor
Sometimes a teacher
Always a student
If you are struggling
Don't be afraid to reach out
I will find you
Even in the darkness
If you are trapped
Under a heavy cloud of pain
I will bring my umbrella
And I promise you
Your weather will change

Grand Utopia

Eating or eating, fuel or food
How are the working class meant to choose
Fat cat stakeholders all millionaires
The system is broken how is this fair

Profits for oil, gas and electric companies
This is totally wrong it can't be okay
Throughout the winter months
People will starve and freeze in the UK

Four-thousand-pound energy bills
For every household in 2023
People won't be able to afford to go to work
Pay bills, feed their families

Grand Utopia what kind of future is this
Only the rich are living in bliss
Will they ever have their day in court
They would, if we, the public insist

Greed and the worst kind of planning
Bringing this once great country to its knees
Our futures look bleak and depressing
This is a spill of a political disease

Parliament is not to be trusted
A house crammed with liars and thieves
They only look after their own interests
Giving speeches filled with lies and deceit

The working-class people are being abused
Where do we go, how does this end
I don't have answers I've only written the truth
Can we pull the plug and all start again.

Take What You Can

(Inspired by Brazilian Jiu Jitsu professor Marc Walder)

Take what you CAN when you CAN
Not what you WANT when you WANT
To live a far more fulfilling life
What you CAN is the reality of truth
In your ability to navigate carefully
What options are genuinely available without cost
What you WANT is a wish, a desire, a fantasy
Something that has not yet formulated
Into a genuine option without risk
How far will your WANT take you to overextend
To put yourself in harm's way

Your egos actions are not formulated without cost
Like someone with no self-control, without foresight
That would consume an entire cake for instance in one sitting
Driven by ego, taking what they WANT
Eating all that is in front of them
Without the ability to consume and digest properly
Having a greater negative impact in a multitude of ways
Aligned with the fact that the cake,
Cannot be enjoyed and digested as it was meant to be

Yet if you can take what you CAN
One slice at a time when served
You can embrace the multitude of ingredients,
flavours and love the cake was made with
All that was put into each slice you can digest
Appreciating it without cost to you
Ready to enjoy the next slice in its entirety
Only when you are ready to consume it
So it is in life, take what you CAN when you CAN
To appreciate all of life's beauty in its entirety
If you take what you WANT when you WANT
You will miss the point of your existence.

Cost of Glory

First place, you have won
The winners circle
Now your new home
The podium awaits
A ceremony for the victorious
You, the guest of honour
Victory
Not a gift earned but hard fought
No quarter given, every inch a war
Doubt crushed; resilience instilled
Indomitable spirit birthed to you and the world

Breath it in, drink it in
Success is to be celebrated
Bask in your glory, revel in victory
Except all the praise
The adulation that comes your way
Dance with arms raised, let it all out
And breathe, for tomorrow is a new day
You start again with the beginners
You will have to earn your stripes
Greatness, needs the hardest worker

The most determined mind
Talent, just a ticket to the start line
After that, the real work begins
The awareness, to come to terms with what victory costs
You must come to terms with the fact all will want you to fail
Starting with you and your self-confidence
You must dismantle all doubt
Your will must destroy any complacency

This is a daily cost
Every second of every minute, of every hour of every day
To be victorious
Sacrifices mount, sacrifices are the daily toll
A heavy price must be paid
To stand alone as the greatest of all time
Have you got what it takes
Only a few ever had
Will your name be spoken in their company
Time will tell.

The Fight

A Symphony of violence
Controlled by the conductor
The instructor
Anyone can filet their limbs in a violent motion
It takes mastery of the mind
Of the body to stay focused
To be in total control
As your opponent loses theirs

In a dance to the bloody death
Your heart rate, that of a top hat
Tapping in emotion
Not the rate of a pounding drum
Your breath icy cold on a winter's morning
Not the painting of a dog in the summer heat
The brain switched into gear
Slowing every action down
Yet your reaction,
Is that of a speeding bullet

Feet light, as not to leave a mark in the sand
Fists at the ready to sting like a cobra strike
Disabling your adversary
The work has already been done
Everything invested
Faculties aligned to work as one
It is time, your time
Ding, Ding round one.

Photos
Top left: Waiting for the judges.
Bottom left: Professor Marc Walder and I.
Top right: Master John Tomlin and I.
Middle right: First place.

Ends of Eternity

I yearn for you always
I dream of you even though I haven't seen you
I haven't heard your voice in decades
A voice that kissed my soul so gently when you spoke to me
My memories of you are just memories now
That I can't quite piece together
Like a favourite song that I cannot find
I have forgotten the title, but I can still hum a few lines
That then reminds me of what it felt like to be in your company
Feeling the power of your aura

You were my jigsaw I could complete in the dark
Knowing every part of you intimately
Clicking the pieces into place just by touch alone
You were intoxicating and your presence still lingers in my mind even
now
The thought of you and I naked together
The fit so perfect that it was meant to be
As if we shared the same heartbeat, we used the same breath in and
out alternately

Every contour of your body shaped by the hands of God himself
Eyes so beautiful that they could undo the work of Medusa, lips so soft
like silk pillows that would support the weariest of heads
Freeing the most troubled of minds of all unhealthy thoughts
A smile that would melt the Antarctic
You were perfection personified
The one thing that never waned even after climax the need only grew
stronger
With every interaction that we shared to be together joined as one

I haven't felt a semblance of that with any other since you
Not in the flesh, not in my mind, not in my heart
Or even the deepest pit of my very soul
My reason for existence taken from me
My purpose on this earth now clouded and unclear
The future is so uncertain, the warmth put out in my heart
The fires of passion doused in misery and pain
All that is left is the space you occupied
Loneliness and an emptiness that will never dissipate
From now until the ends of eternity.

Black Suit

I dread getting this out of the closet
It's something I hate to wear
I have to keep up appearances
A lot of people are going to be there

My white shirt's starched and gleaming
I always iron my tie
I'll make my shoes look like mirrors
I pause, to let out a deep sigh

Black pants and socks on my bed
After I've showered, I'll put them on
A quick glance at my watch, it's time
I'd better be getting along

Tucking my shirt in to my trousers
Feeding my belt around my waist
Putting a handkerchief in my top pocket
I shouldn't need it but I'll take it in case

I front of the mirror I put on my black tie
Not too tight, I want to breathe
Another sigh, I think I've got everything
I don't want to but it's time to leave

I will see friends I've not seen in a while
Family members I hardly ever see
I wish I did not have to go the funeral
But I will, he'd do the same for me

I put on my black jacket and button it up
I am dressed with tears in my eyes
Wallet and keys, I lock the front door
It's time to go and say goodbye.

The Meaning

What is the meaning of life, billions have pondered this question since the Stone Ages yet the answer still alludes us to this day.
What is it that makes life meaningful, fulfilling and whole, could it be knowledge of self, service to fellowman, prayer, devotion to God, devotion to family.

Many cultures will point you in many different directions for the answer to leading a meaningful life and what makes life meaningful. We can look as far as the heavens for some insight into this age-old question, when in-fact the answer may lay within everyone's being.

What makes a life whole, what events, experiences and actions are required, giving life meaning, having purpose and a fulfilled existence. Is it your ability to be kind, to love completely, unconditionally, to give so much more than you will ever receive.
To sacrifice yourself to save another, to teach and impart your wisdom to the young and needy. To be humble, to praise others, lift the spirits of the suffering.

To give hope to those that feel hopeless, to love, teach and share your meaning of love to all, even those that may have committed the most horrendous crimes. To forgive the unforgivable. All these actions and gestures, over the course of a lifetime would give it meaning.

Yet that still does not answer the age-old question, what is the meaning of life, perhaps it is not a question to be answered by others. Each of us must look within ourselves for answers,
I am sure happiness, joy, love and the ability to forgive,
are just a few of the necessary ingredients to make your life meaningful, the rest is up to you.

Hoarding

No one understands my plight
I love everything I own
Wall to sealing I fill the space
To feel safe within my home
Newspapers, clothes and food shopping
Possessions mean the world to me
I am judged by those with no understanding
A hoarder is all they ever see

You don't know my history
Or what I've lived through
I share my home with shame and guilt
You have no idea, do you
I have a relationship with all my belongings
Each items, comfort and support
I see fingers pointing and judging eyes
You don't know the battles I've fought

You think I'm dirty and disgusting
Rubbish and junk, that's all you see
I would be exposed and vulnerable
If you took my possessions from me
Please show a little compassion
I haven't been outside in years
I've built this fortress for protection
To allay me from all my fears

So many things I have sacrificed
To calm the voices in my head
From friendships, love and family
To bathing and sleeping in my bed
They want to repossess my home
Labelled a hoarder, I have no voice
I am being forced to bin my possessions
How am I expected to make that choice

Please don't come in all guns blazing
Tread softly making your way to me
Already loaded with embarrassment and shame
I need unconditional love and empathy

Please show me a little compassion
Hoarding feels like it's now a crime
I need your support and patience
For me to heal will take some time.

Beauty

What is it to be beautiful
What do I need to see
Having a semblance of what real beauty is
I must have some inside of me
Is beauty a song in the morning
Being sung from the birds in the trees
Is it to watch them in full flight
That's so beautiful to see
Is beauty a smile from a stranger
An embrace from friends without need
A kindness that cannot be repaid
Being selfless is beautiful to see

Is beauty the perfect love song
A conversation from lost ones so dear
Close your eyes, hear their voices
Beautiful, heart-warming and clear

Is beauty a new born baby
In the wild able to run free
Or an old couple still hand in hand
That's a beautiful sight indeed
Is beauty the ability to plant a seed
To nurture and love it with all you know
To put your heart and soul into it
Taking pride in watching it grow
What's beautiful is different for all of us
Our examples we can each share
No need to look far if that's what you seek
As beauty is everywhere.

The Hour

I see you standing on an icy lake
I can hear the ice beginning to crack
How have you ended up out there I wonder
I'll find out as you make your way back

I cannot come out to save you
The ice would break, we would both drown
I can support and encourage you
Listen to my voice and follow its sound

My impulse is to rescue you
The next time I might not be here
If I encourage you to find your confidence
You'd have the strength to battle your fears

That's why this job is extremely important
So much can happen within the magical hour
Counsellors, mindful of thoughts and feelings
It's the client we must work to empower

This is the role of the counsellor
Whether by zoom in person or phone
Listen support and empower our clients
So they have all that's required to survive on their own.

Hug

Something as simple as a hug
Showing that you really care
Feeling warm and supported
If events seem too much to bare

You hug sometimes to say hello
You hug sometimes to say goodbye
Whether overjoyed or heartbroken
You hold them if they need to cry

When sad news lands at the door
A hug can reassure it's gonna be alright
When you haven't seen a loved one
You squeeze and hold them tight

That connection is priceless
It speaks volumes without words
When you really need support
Your emotions will feel heard

If little ones fall and hurt themselves
In your arms they want to be
Hold them, they'll know it's okay
And no more tears will you see

Do not underestimate its power
It is the purest form of love
Put your arms around one another
Enjoy the wonders of a hug.

I Can See

I wonder if you realise
I can read you like a book
This act isn't fooling anybody
One look was all it took
Pretending you're empathetic
That you really care
People's feelings aren't a game
It's not truth or dare
When your audience isn't watching
Your devil can't resist
The real you comes out to play

With the stage name, narcissist
When you're living two truths
Then one must be a lie
You don't have to say a word
The answer's written in your eyes
Aren't you getting tired
Pointing fingers, alluding blame
Having the capacity to be much more
But you won't and that's a shame

People like you are dangerous
Causing damage that can't be repaired
Can't you see the harm you do
Or don't you even care
How can I warn others
To be mindful, so they see
What your real intentions are
From their perspective, that's the key

My influence is not needed
Aspersions, I don't need to cast
You will be your own undoing
This act will never last
As with all things fake in life
You will get found out in the end
Think before you act in future
And some bridges you might mend.

Back to The Start

How have I ended up here
Being single and all alone
I'm too old to start again
I dread living on my own

I thought I had found the one
I loved him, he loved me too
I felt like I had died inside
When he told me we were through

I built my life around this man
I gave him everything and more
For him to leave the way he did
Burned me to the core

What do I tell my family,
How can I face our friends
I will have to go over what happened
Again, and again and again

I just feel like an empty shell
What more could I have done
I must come to terms with the fact
For him I'm not the one.

Selfish

Is it ever your fault
Are you ever to blame
You don't seem to care
Don't you have any shame
The chaos you cause
The havoc you wreak
The damage is permanent
Is that what you seek
Are you oblivious
To the hurt that you cause

So self-absorbed
No thought to pause
Unbelievably selfish
Your only focus is you
Collateral damage
It's a thing that you do
The excuses you make
Justifying the stunts that you pull
Defending the indefensible

You're nobody's fool
Other people's feelings
Are not your concern
To get what you want
You'd watch the world burn
What about those closest
The ones that you love
A minor distraction
That's still not enough
Your tunnel vision
Matched with a heart of stone

You are financially successful
But you'll be toasting alone
There's still time to mend bridges
If you'd just open your eyes
See the truth in your actions
That have been hidden by lies

If you continue on this path

Not stopping to reflect
Continuing the destruction
Of selfish neglect
You will be lonely
Bitter and twisted through
A face of regret in the mirror
Will be crying at you
Your future's not set
Yet your times losing sand
Don't leave it for too long
It's still in your hands.

Be Careful What You Wish For

Be careful what you wish for
Thinking dreams come true
Only after you can't turn back
You find they weren't meant for you
Loves in the eye of the beholder
Put heart and soul into what you see
Players will only ever play games
For self-preservation let them be

Watch for those without loyalty
Like hunters separating the pack
If they separate you from your love
You might never get them back
The grass is never greener
With those taking time to love and care
Busy loving what they've nurtured
To waste time looking elsewhere
Wandering eyes will never settle
They will only ever roam
Unstable foundations have no future
They won't make a happy home

What comes around goes around
Even if it takes a little time
If you lose someone you love
You face a life sentence for the crime
A few verses from a stranger
Can pull a heartstring or two
It's your journey of life and love
The narrative's up to you.

Grounding

These are just poems
They're not about you
You may have been impacted
That's what poems can do
So take a deep breath
Hold it for two
Then let it out
Let's work to ground you
Repeat this sequence
You are in a safe space
Lighten the load
Feel the smile on your face
The warmth in your heart
Concentrate on its beat
Wiggle your toes
In your shoes feel your feet

The back of your legs
Pressed up against the chair
Take a deep breath
You're getting there
Tension's leaving your shoulders
Feel your muscles relax
Repeat the sequence
Focus now on your back
With complete concentration
Feel your bum in the chair
Checking in on your body

It's a great form of self-care
Breathe out again
That's it, hold it for two
Then breath in, fill your lungs
Your body's now calming you
You're getting there slowly
Letting this process begin
Now feeling positive
More centred within
Release the tension
Feel your body relax
You're now feeling grounded
There you go, welcome back.

Acknowledgements

To Joanne Williams thank you deeply for your love and support over these many years. Many thanks to a very special woman, Annette Kent and Vince Russell for the magnificent work and fabulous ideas for Triggers.

To Glen, Danny, Mark, Mat, Bradley, Dean, Rachael, Dave and Paul this journey, my life, would not have been the same without your love, support, and friendships. Special mention to Ann Smythe and Pat Williams, Glen Colins, Craig Holland and wife to be Amy, Dave and Aggie Merrilees and Richard and Liz and Ray.

Mentions to: Margaret Kennedy, Lisa Bari, Rebecca Topham Roche, Rachel Tansy Chadwick, Keith Bray, Hannah Stanislaus, Chloe Smith, Lee Cambell, Leeanne Saunders, Ann Stack, Rodrig Andrisan, Tony Lewis, Jason and Paula Richards, Lalah Bushen, Danielle Tillett, Lisa Rackham, Stacey Moreland, Daniel Pang, Nicky Howroyd, Karen Rushbrook, Jo McBride, Kathy Mitton, Chris Cooper, Circe Powell and Sean Faulkner you have all over the course of my life pushed me to be better and do better.

Marc Walder my BJJ instructor and teacher on the mats and in life, thank you, you have been a huge inspiration to me. John Tomlin, Kieran Mackey, Darren Comins my Karate instructors and friends, thank you. Carrie, Keeleigh, and Kiran, you continue to inspire, keep up the magnificent work.

A huge thank you to Jon Wilson Cooper, Michelle, Debra, Gemma and my supervisor Jane Cooper. All classmates of 2021/22 and 2022/23 at The Albany Centre studying Gestalt Therapy, I am grateful for the support, love and inspiration provided throughout the academic years, special mention to Shahin Manji, Caroline Madsen and Brendan Smith I love you all dearly.

Thank you, Stephen Higgins, for allowing the use of the beautiful photo you took State Side, (being the Front Cover no less).

Dolly Drake I inherited the gift of poetry from you, Don Drake thank you for teaching me what it takes to be a gentleman, I love you both always and forever.

I would like to say very special thank you to Kathryn Ward, without the time help and support you gave me at Citylit, my Counselling and Poetic journeys would have ended before they even began, I am heading in the right direction in my life thanks to you.

Lastly a huge thank you to my counsellor Pam provided by the NHS in 2017 those sessions changed my life.

Printed in Great Britain
by Amazon

30116920R10077